The photographs are printed without any editing or adjustment other than a corrective exposure for consistency of publication. Nothing has been changed in the photographs since the day, September 14, 2001 they were taken in NYC from the window of my 2000 JEEP SE Wrangler that had just returned from taking me cross country photographing the beauty, bravery, love and lives of everyday Americans. The JEEP, like my cameras, had by then become an enhancement of myself and soul in much the same way a person adapts to a prosthetic device designed to compensate but for us "Bio-mechanical humans" make our lives and art greater than ever before.

Nothing has been changed. Nothing. The billboards and signs are exactly as they were on that day and probably as they were on 911. Photographers often go for the "money shots". There are many. As I said, I cannot shoot tragedy. These aren't the "money shots" but they are the hardworking love shots. I am happy with that. I capture with my camera the bravery, strength, love and life of American, indeed of humanity, who have persevered through disaster and gone on, who survive and eventually thrive. That's what humanity does. It experiences disasters, picks themselves up and goes on. New York City has always been an inspiration for humanity all over the world overcoming the worst of times. That's because New Yorkers come from all over the world. The book is merely one story in that inspiration and it is beautiful to me because it was written by the city herself.

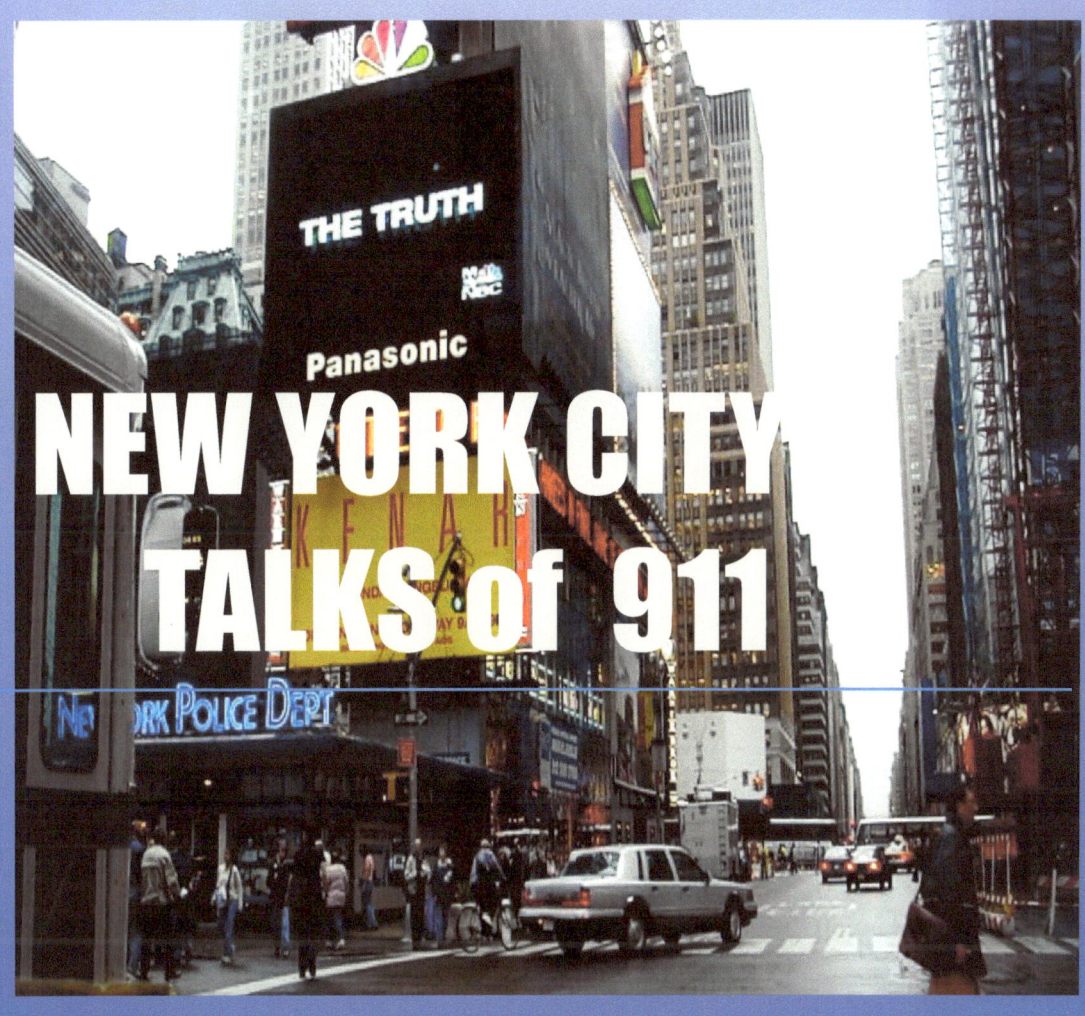

A Photo essay of New York City taken right after The city tells its own story in those amazing true photographs. You always knew New Yorkers were strong. Sometimes that strength shows itself in a grandmother sending her grandchild to school just days after 911 and waiting on a street corner in the rain for the child to return from school just blocks from the disaster. That is strength. That is New York.

Photographer and Author Donna White-Davis weary of seeing the World Trade Center story presented with the towers going down over and over again in news broadcast. She felt the true story would be found by driving her Jeep though New York and recording with photographs the resilience of New York city three days after the worst disaster in the history of the city.

I went to New York City to see if I could help. I quit my therapist position on 9/11. I had just returned from driving cross country photographing America and falling in love with the people of our country. I focus on the good, the beautiful, Empire State Games, the athletic, the mountains, small towns and big cities, the music venues of America, the Rodeos and the Fairs. I cannot photograph disasters. A local newspaper asked me once. I said "No, you see my portfolio. I only photograph the beauty."

I had spent the days after 911 watching the towers going down over and over in newsreels and felt with a deep emotion hard to explain that that destruction caused by the others to New York was not the story. New Yorkers are strong. I knew that. I am a New Yorker. That destruction was not the story.

While driving across country and going through many of the cities of America with music venues I came to realize that cities greet you with their own messages displayed across billboards and neon signs or sounded from the radio stations playing their style. The cities talked to me as I entered them. I knew New York had something to say. I went to New York to hear New York's story.

I entered the city on 8th Ave under the elevated train and travelled out from under it onto Broadway and followed Broadway to the 911 site. At each stoplight I photographed exactly what New York was saying to me, to all of us. Here is her story.

Donna White-Davis

*When I arrived in New York City it
was raining and I chose to photograph
through the windows of my JEEP. It
was as if the entire city was weeping.
Yet through the tears people were
getting up, going to work, shopping,
and the stores and restaurants were
like bouquets left to say*

"We care, we miss them."

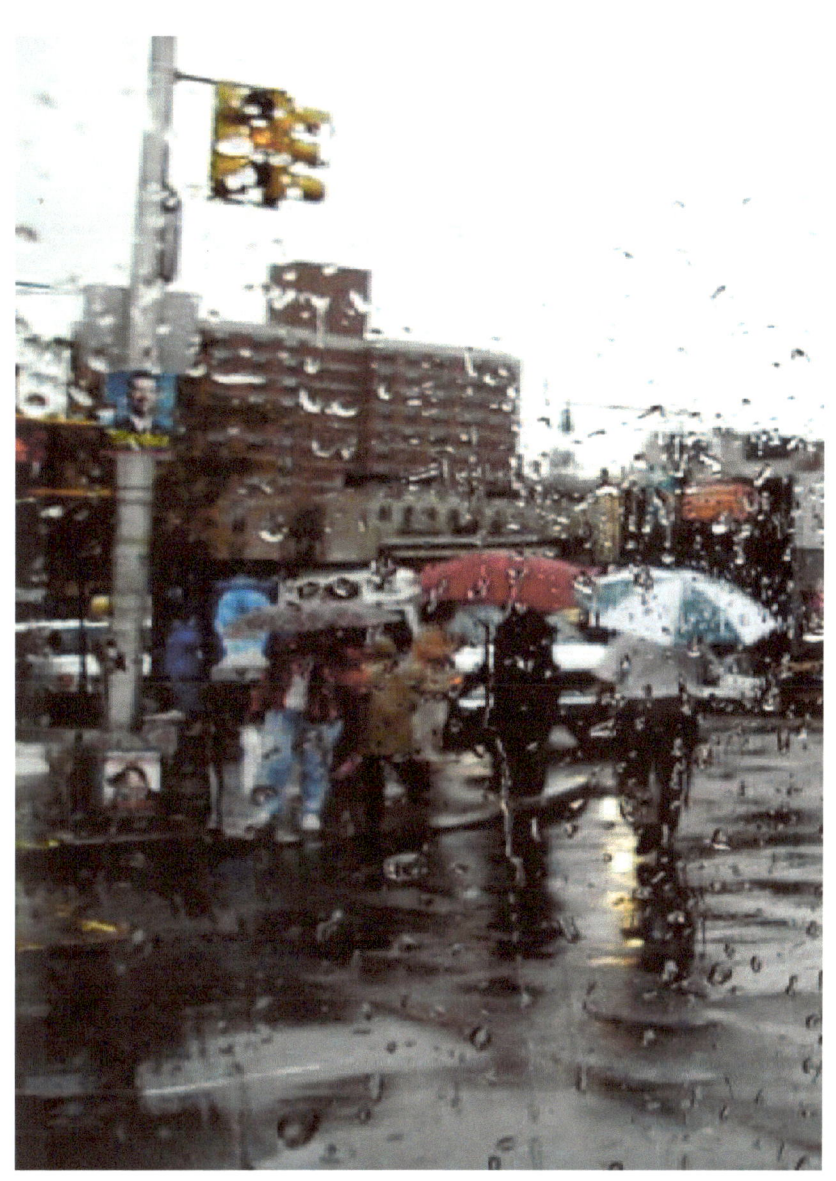

I rode under the elevated trains, the rumble echoing overhead, used to be a bit frightening to me but not now it, too, had been humbled. I chose to stay there to feel the vibrations and hear the noise, to imagine an echo of the tragedy.

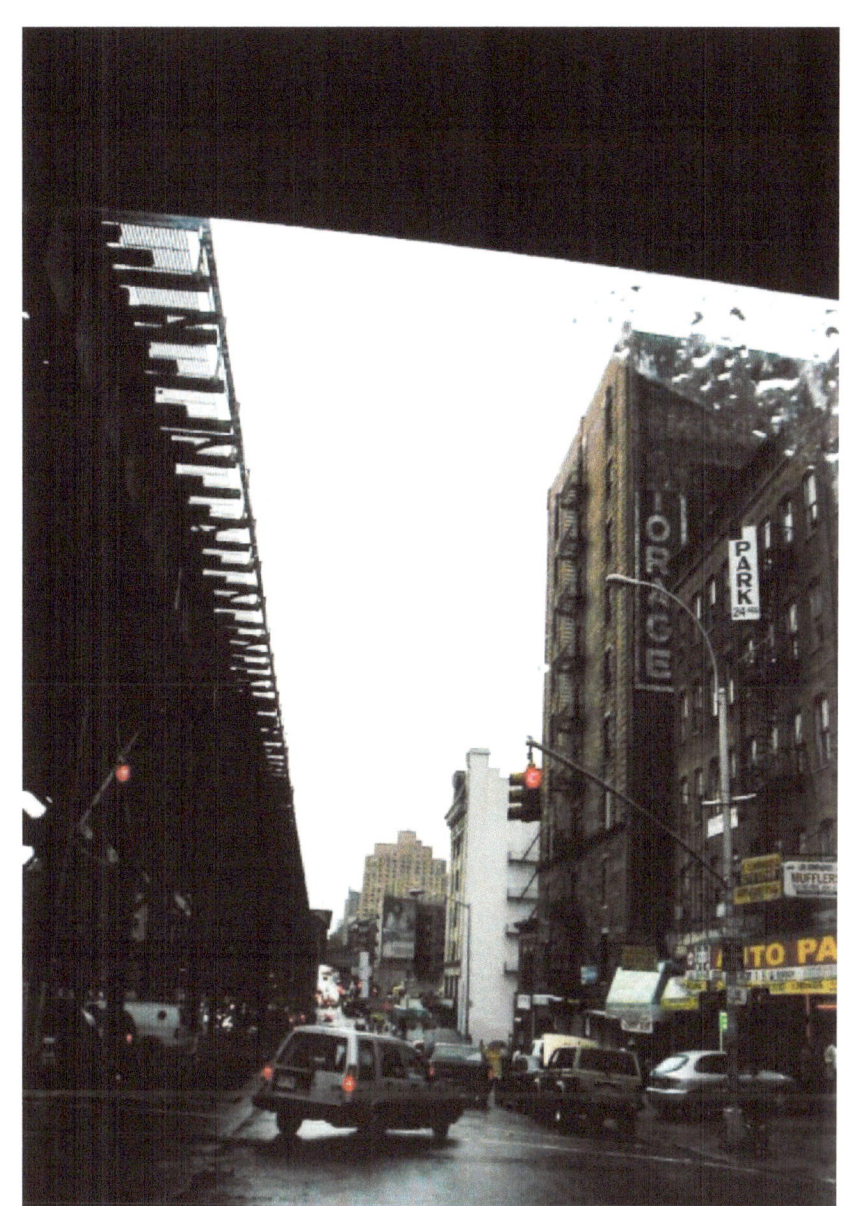

Bicyclists came from all directions, ignoring the rain as if nothing would stop them, escorting my drive on Broadway.

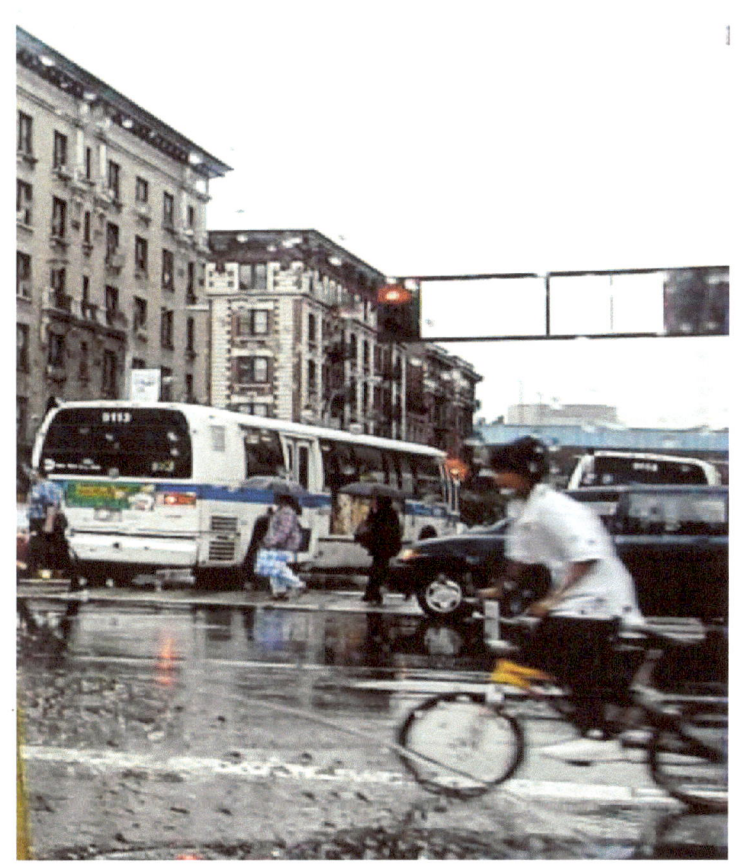

Young, old, playing, working all cycling in the rain through the traffic, through the city, reminding us of why the city became peaceful in the first place, why she will become peaceful once again.

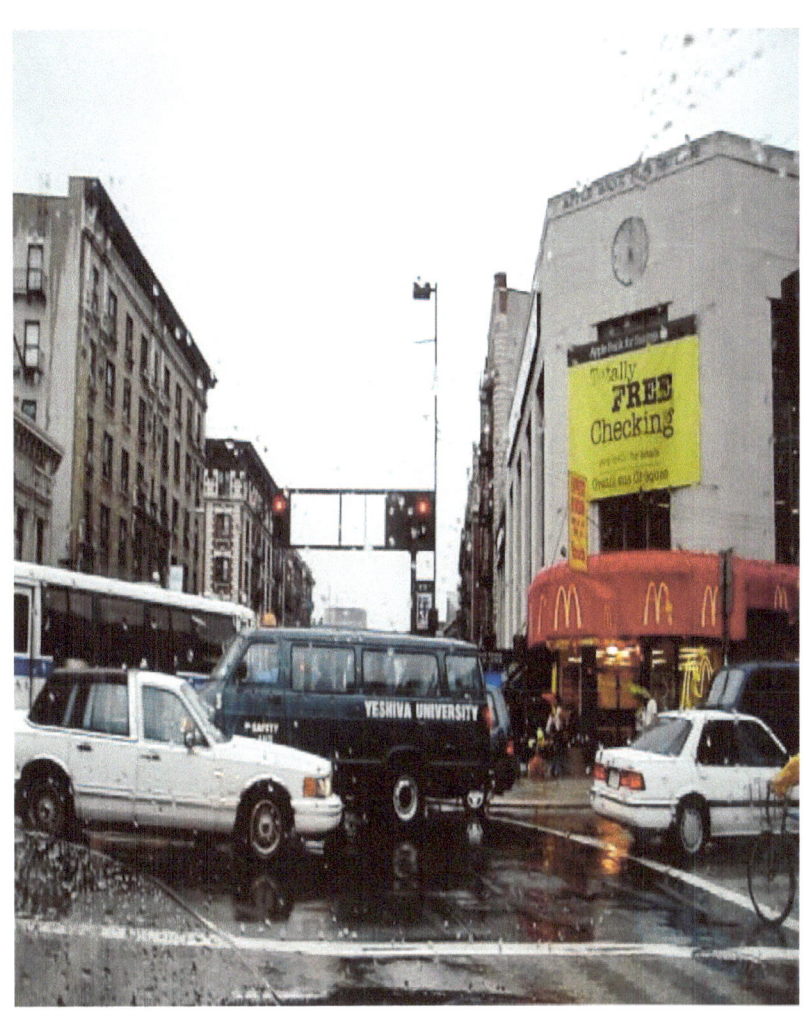

The neighborhoods passed by each with their languages, and their signs, and their aromas, and the beauty, even now, even today, even in this rain. They blended their gardens after the storm.

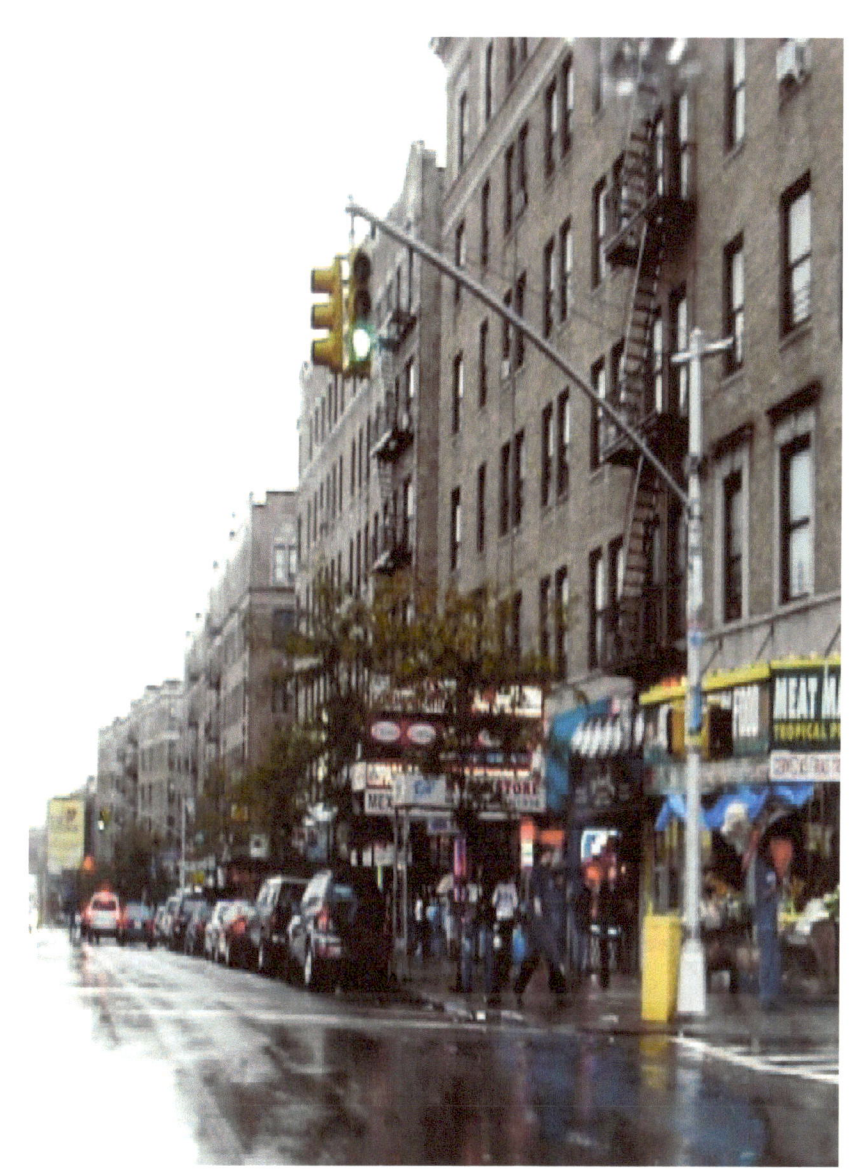

The buses plowed a path, filled with working New Yorkers as if to say "We'll show you what happened to us. Go slow. It may hurt you." Like a man returning from an operation, recovering but fraile and protective of the wound.

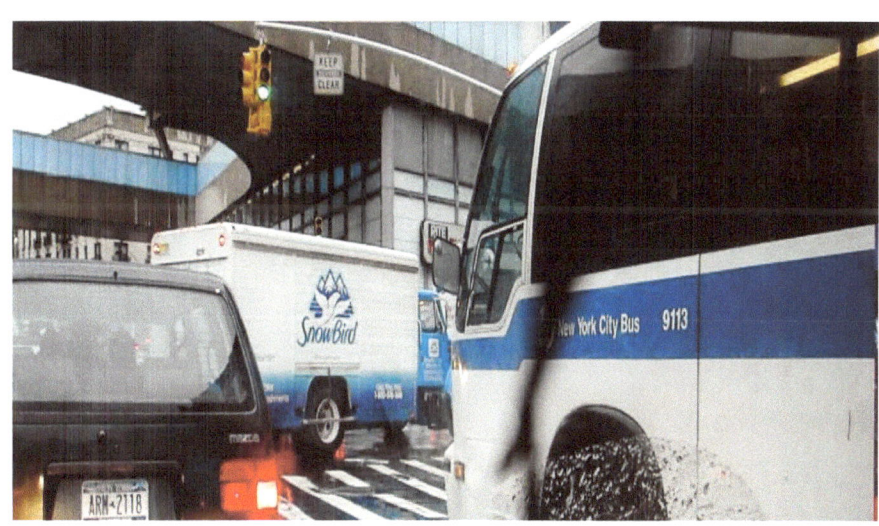

The rain began to clear a bit, as sorrow
lifts, mistily, lingering in one's heart.
The other buildings rose in my view,
buildings formerly cowed by the WTC
and now looking like precious jewels
we have to protect instead of places we
ran into for protection from the rain.

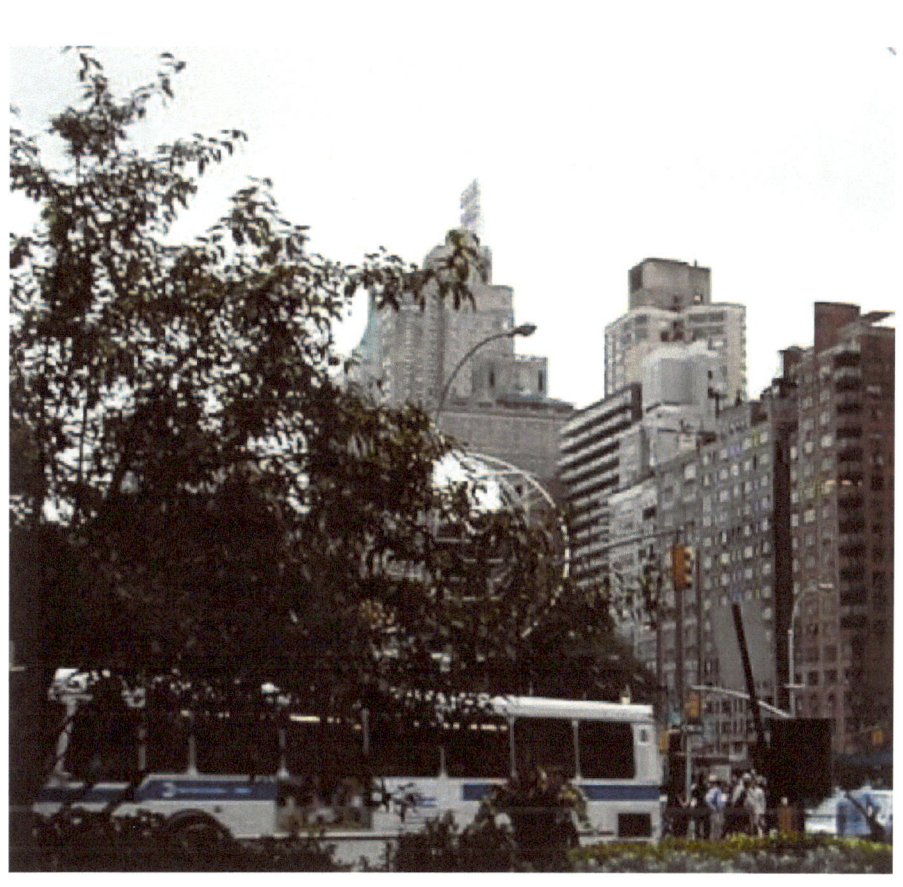

Lots of umbrellas everywhere, popping up to share, covering daughters, sons, moms, dads, sisters, brothers, Becoming a strong and reassuring cover even after the disaster just three days and blocks away.

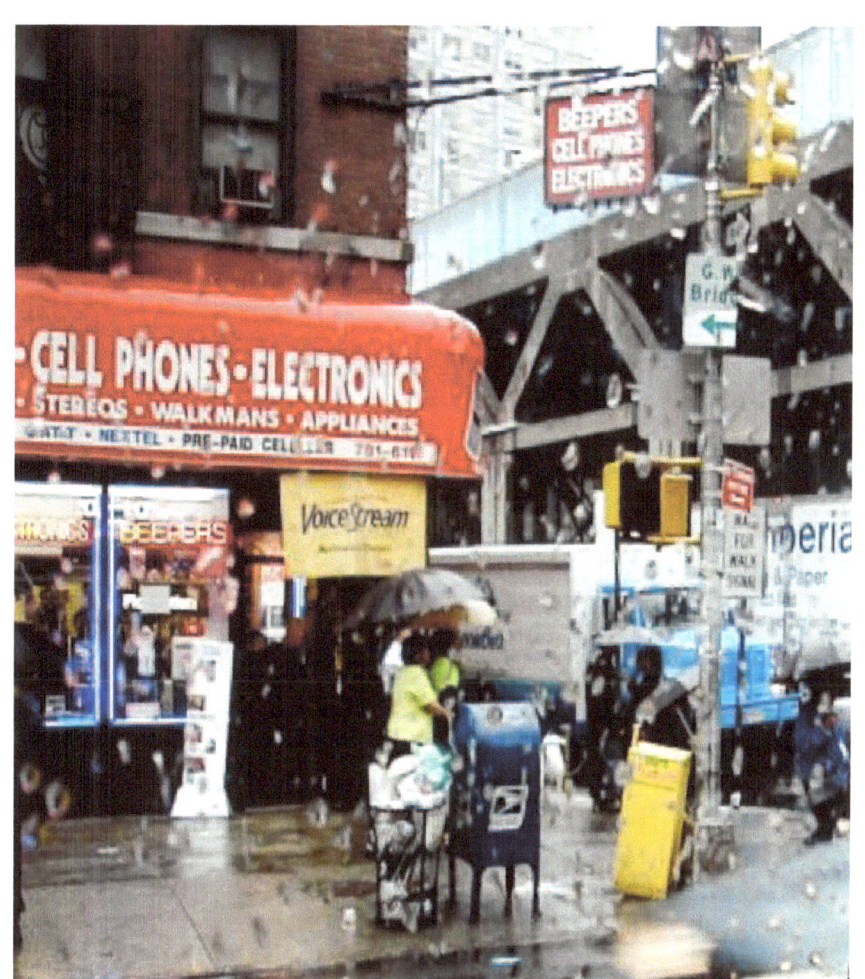

People everywhere walking around just like at home, just like anywhere in America, unafraid. It wasn't TV looking for the sensational, the biggest, the worst, showing over and over the headline tragedy.

It was life and it was strong and it was going on.

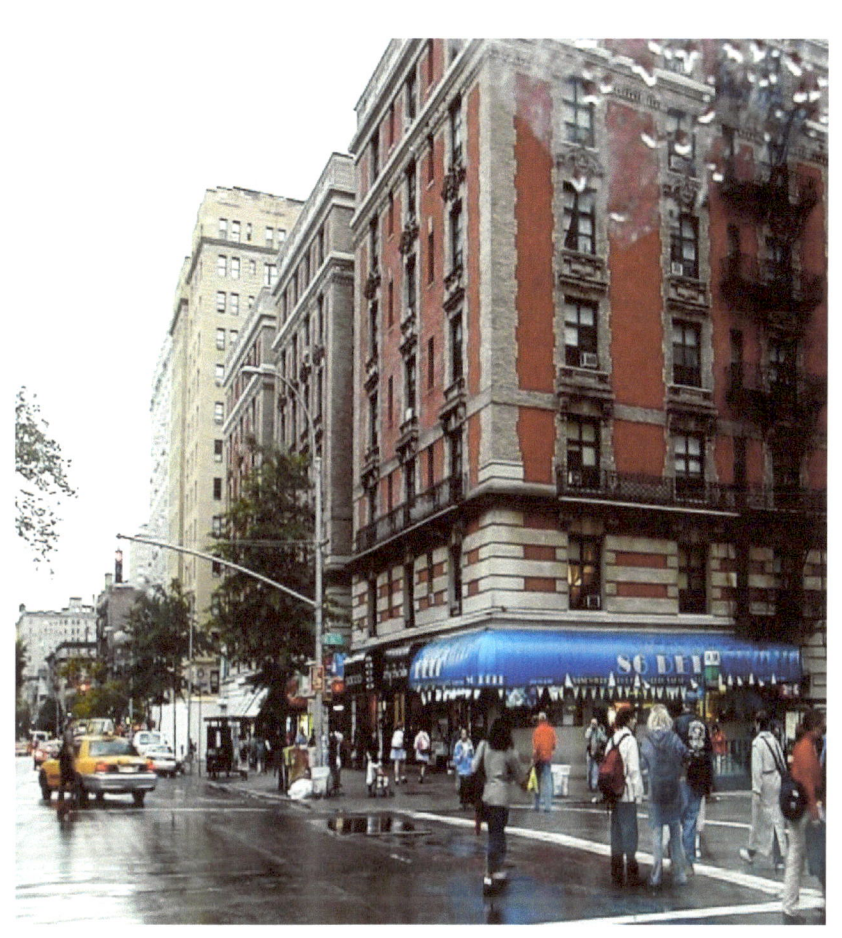

Buildings before obscured, now shown,

reflecting the crisis.

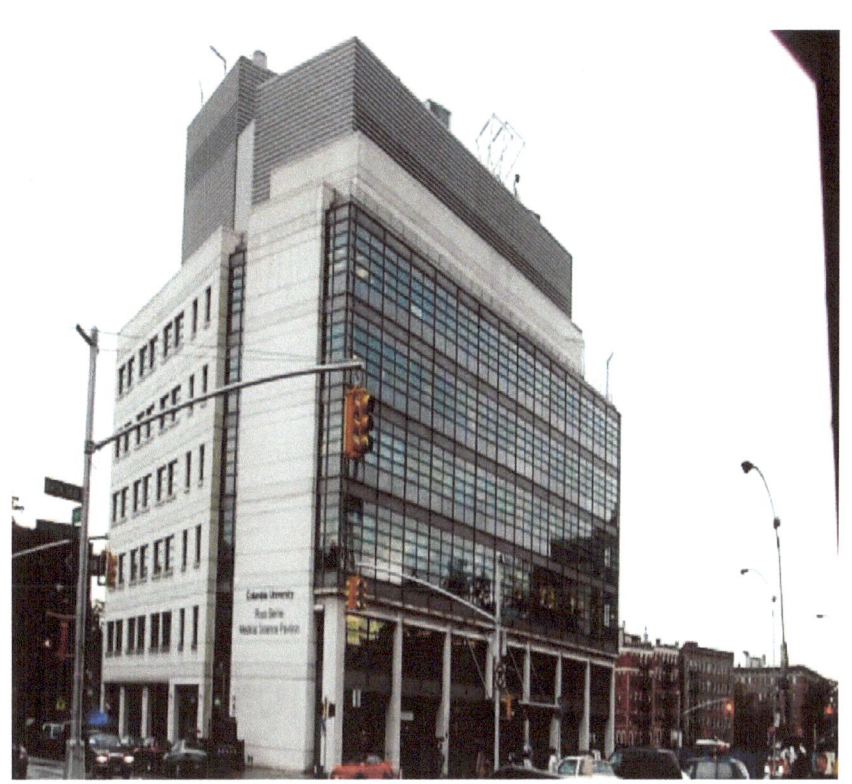

Normal street corners, with normal people, doing normal things and only blocks away, the worse devastation. Strength and courage sometimes comes in the everyday things like being brave enough to send your child to school only days away from the tragedy.

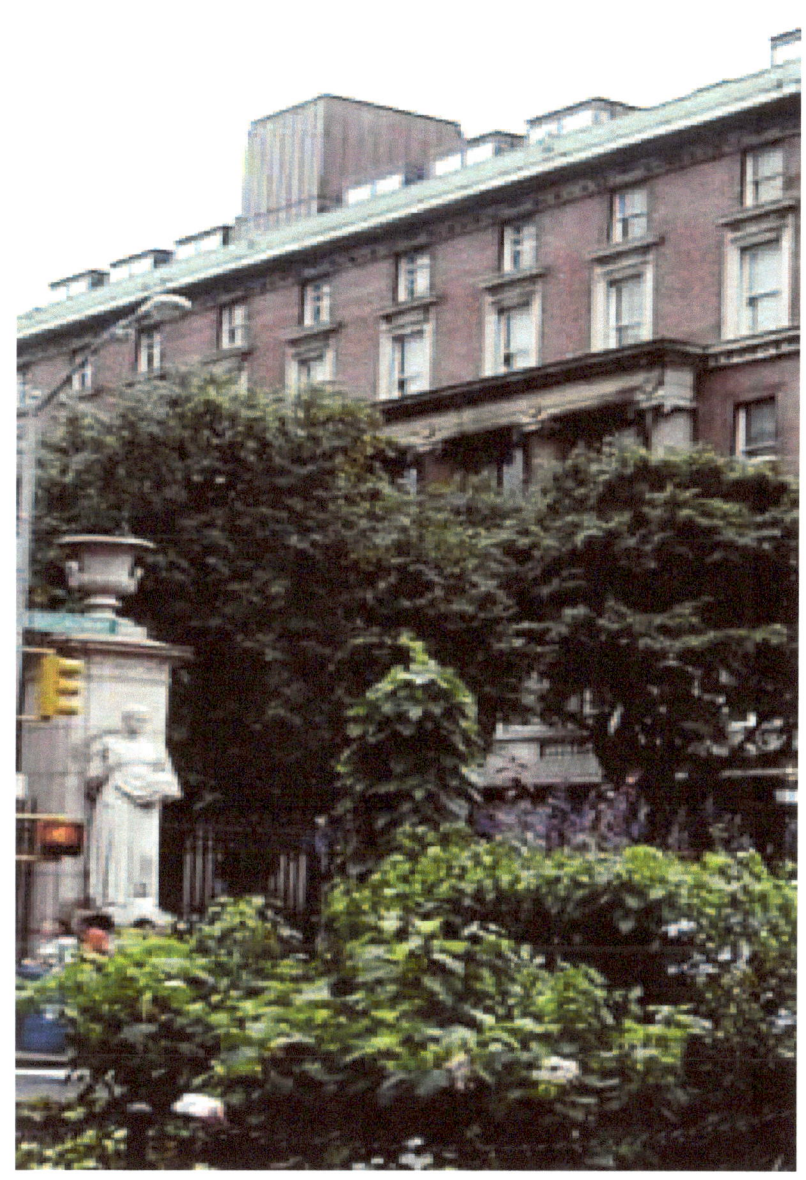

*The awnings sheltering from the rain,
so fragile a shelter that always seemed
enough had to be enough even today.*

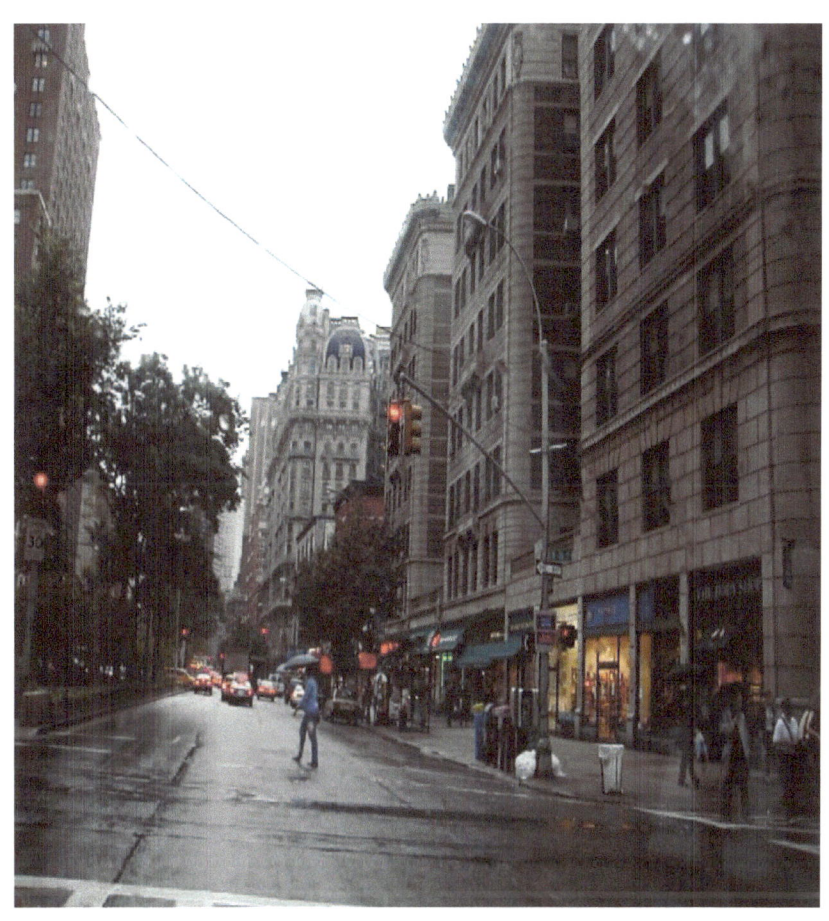

The essentials being done while the unthinkable had been done and the unbelievable was going on just blocks away and New Yorkers go on.

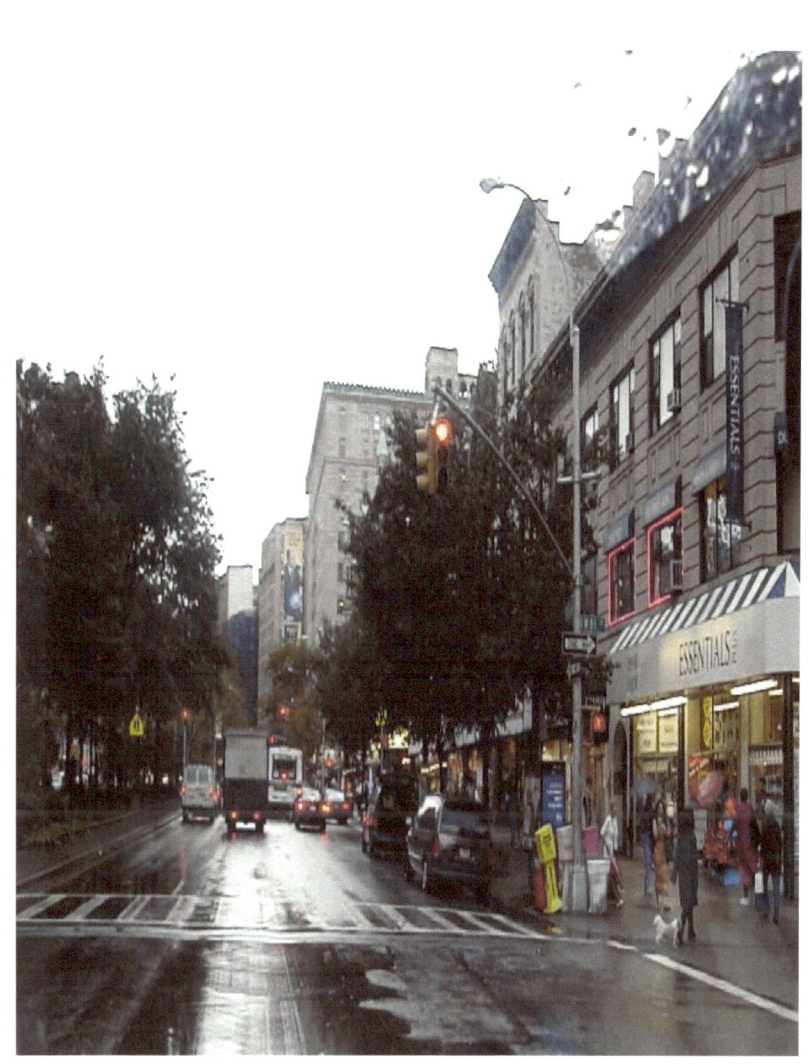

As you pass, the shops become elegant and the neighborhood starts holding memories as the street numbers pass the window. The leather backpacked student in the mini-skirt, the director in the park carriage filming, quiet rest on the rock by the lake to write in what was then the peace of the newly calmed city. New York was quiet except for the subway and, now the construction machinery forced to deconstruct.

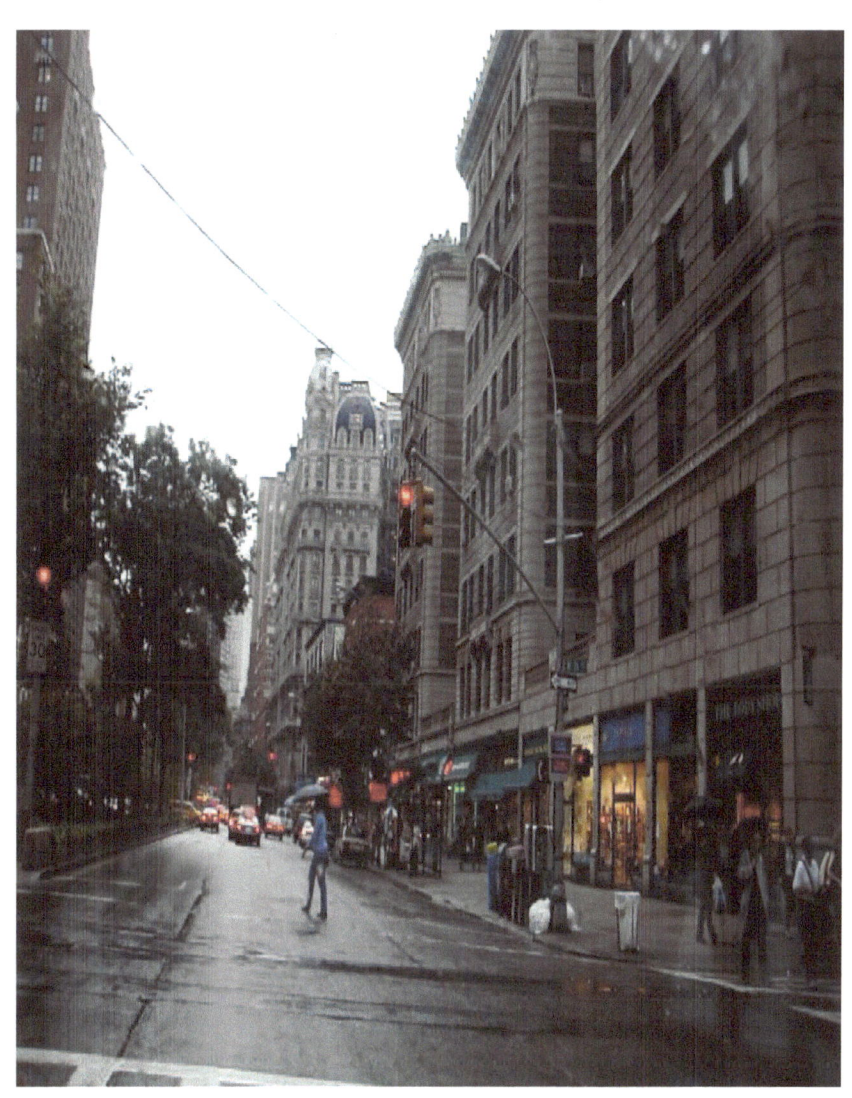

Taxis, buses and advertisements for flight, all part of the hub of America's heart, suddenly being redesigned but there ,that day, as all days, there alive in New York City the possibility of being the same each and every day. New Yorkers wanting that so much and knowing that it would never be the same, it had been harmed and now it would have to recover peace.

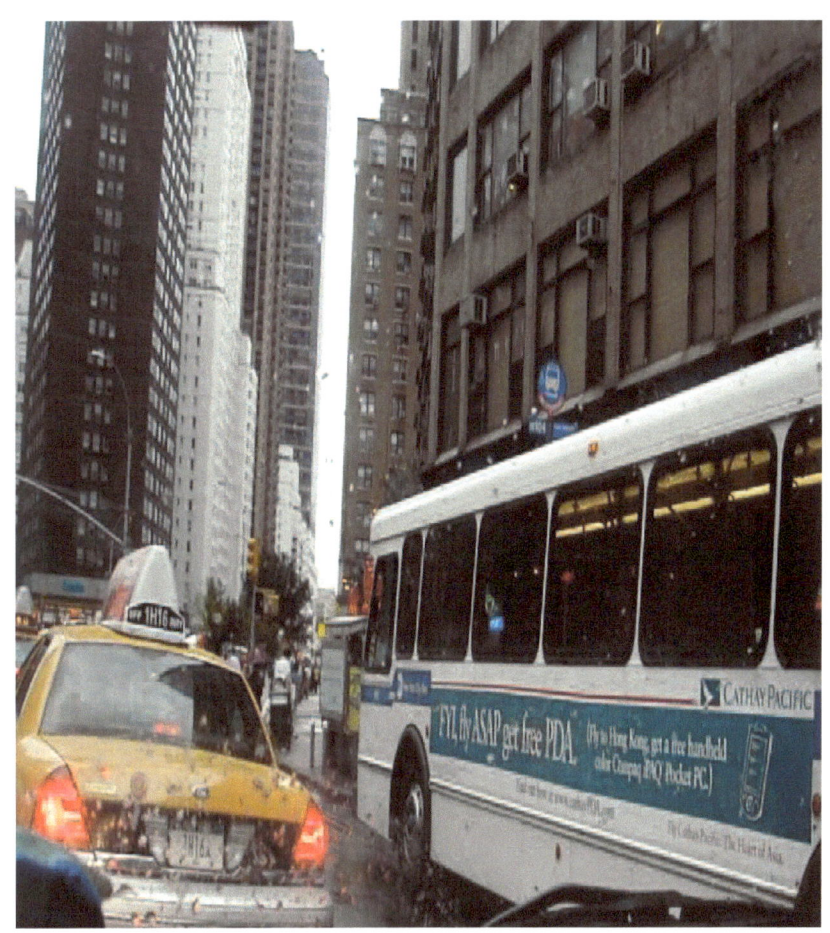

The other buildings sprouted into

the Broadway skyline as if to say

"Look at me."

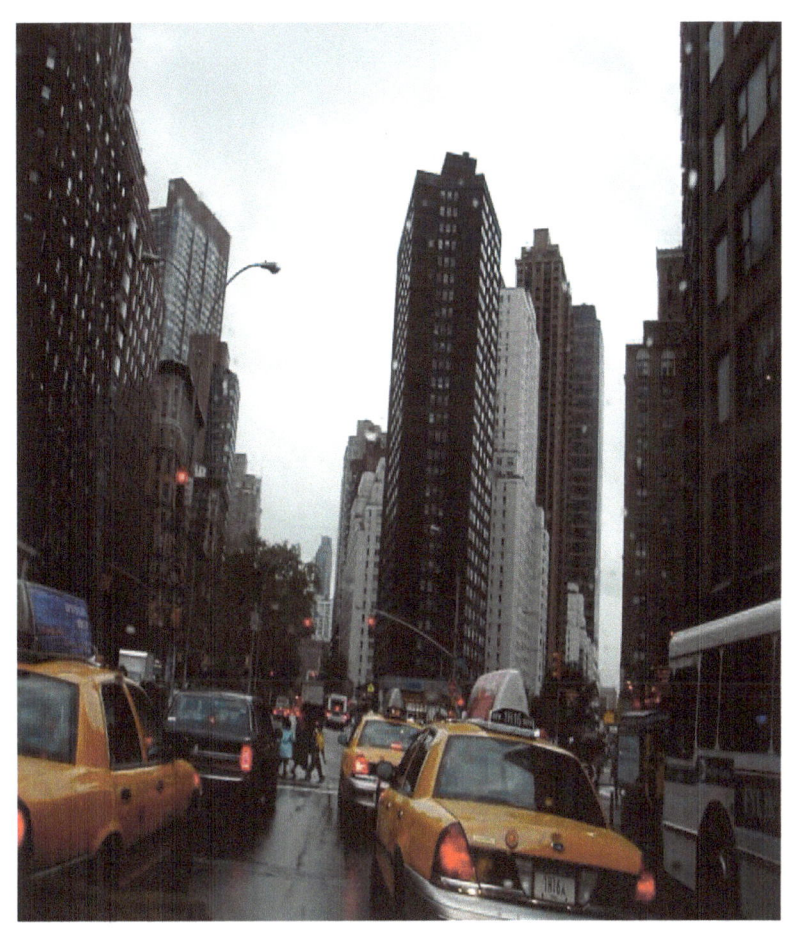

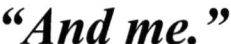

"And me."

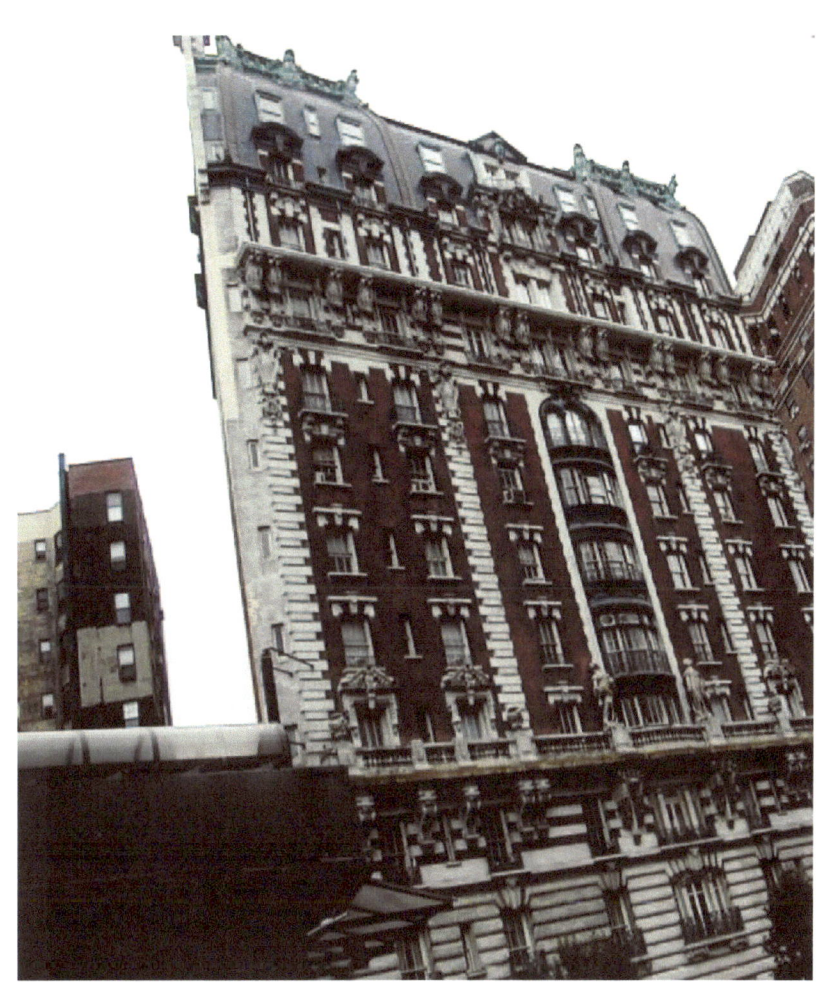

"And me."

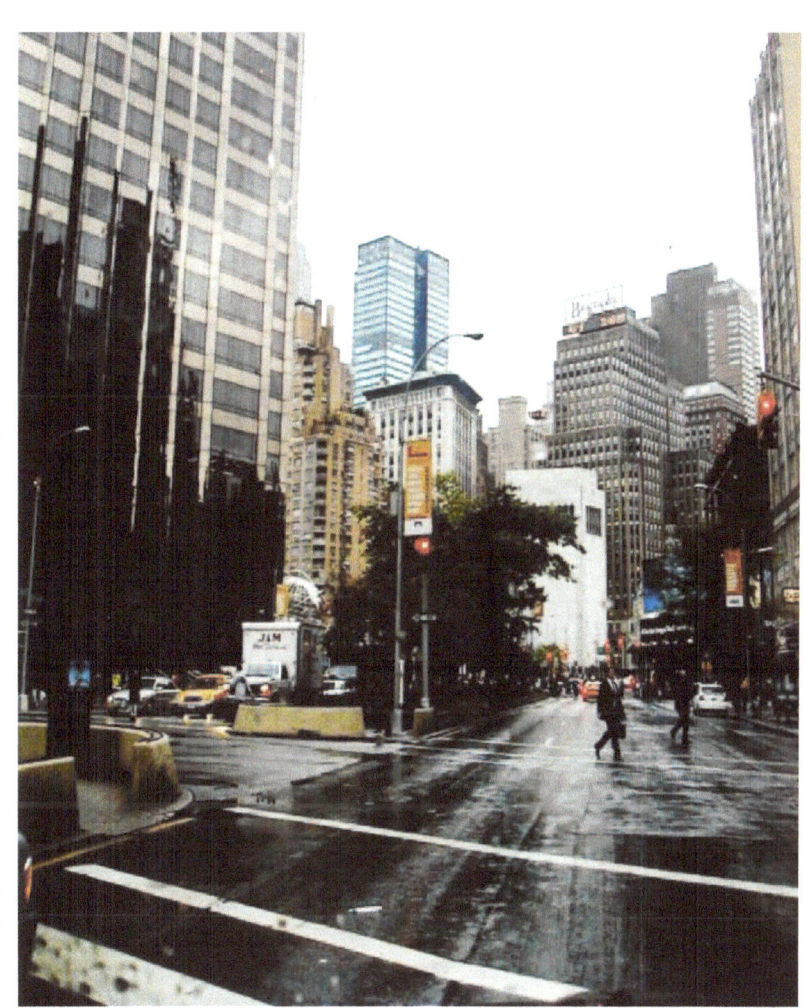

"Choose any of us like the friends of a lost husband would offer to comfort the grieving wife. I am there for you. I know I won't replace them but I am there."

And it is received with the same grateful yet non-accepting feeling. There are no replacements for deep loss.

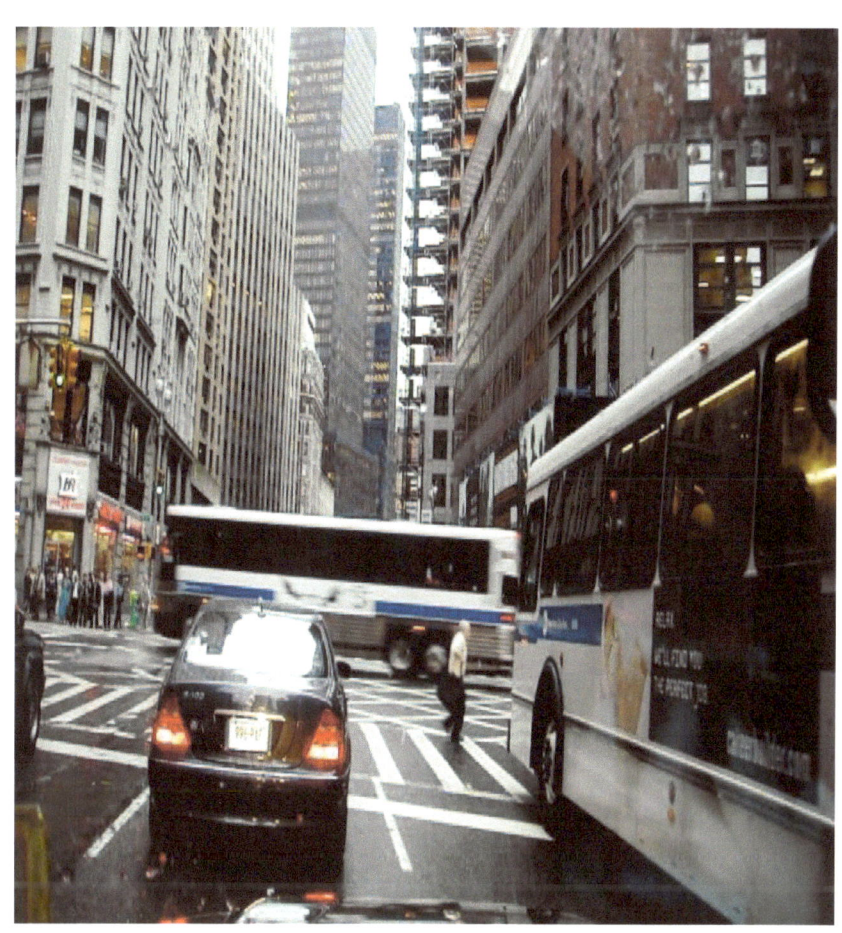

The billboards themselves

gave their own sermon of promise.

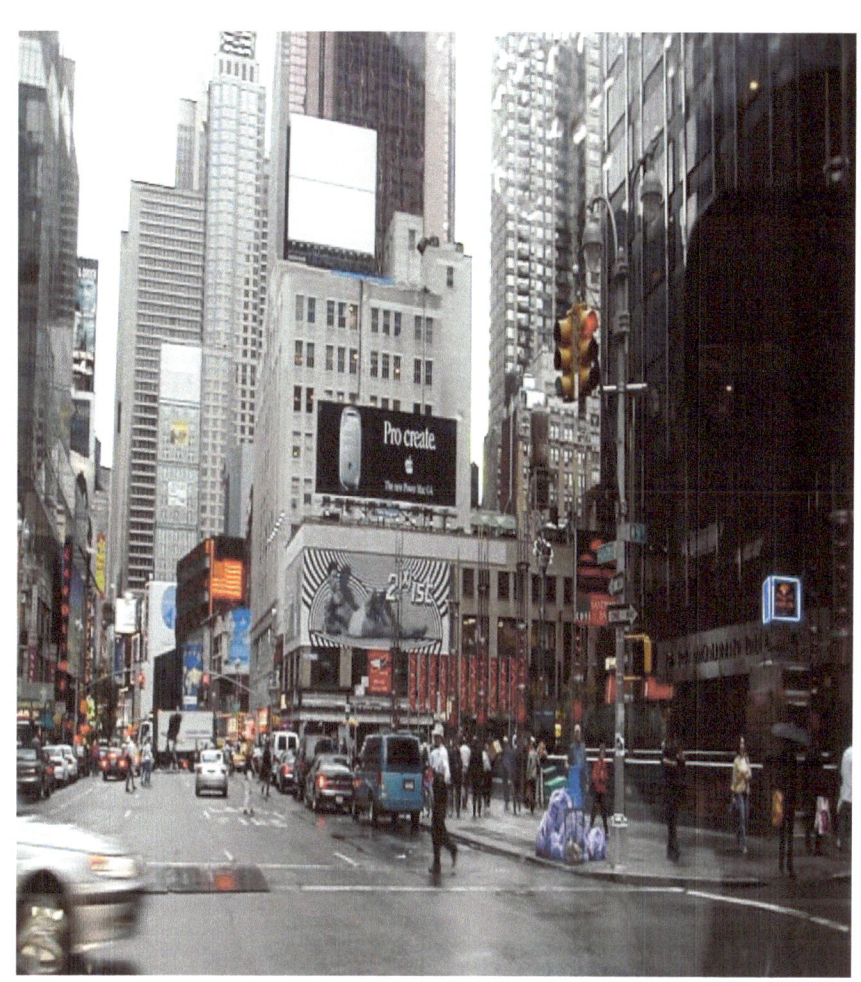

And implored God for the answers.

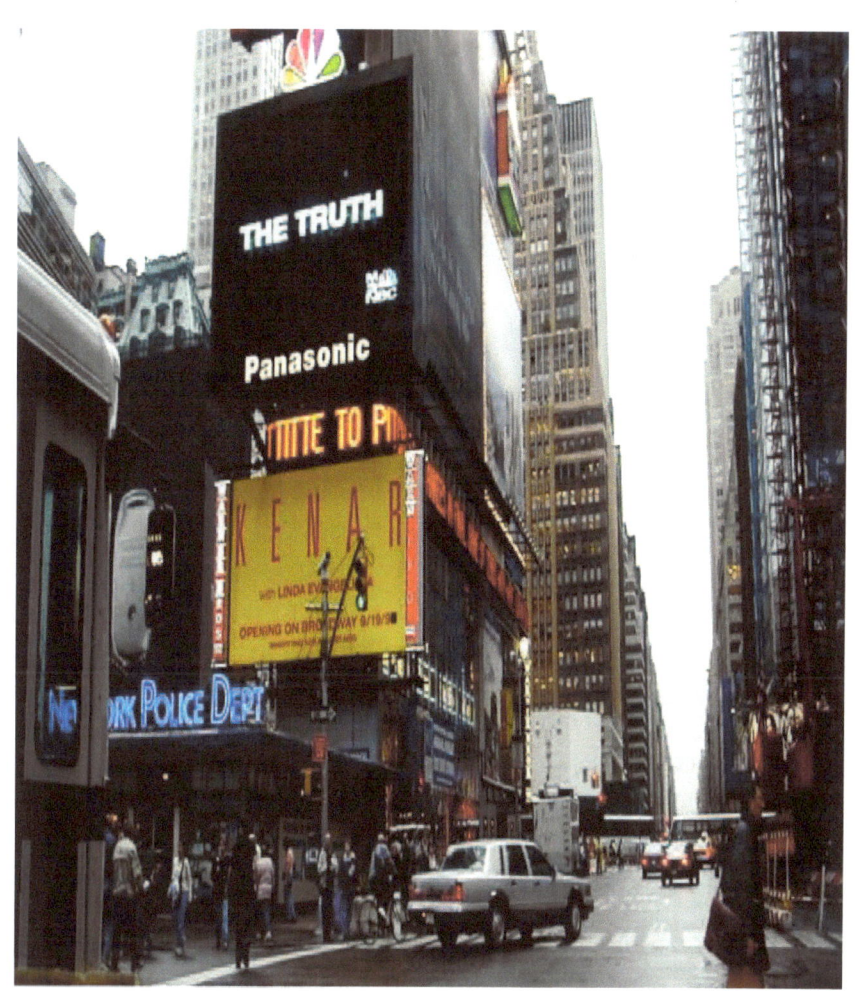

And the people went home from working, and school, and volunteering, and praying.

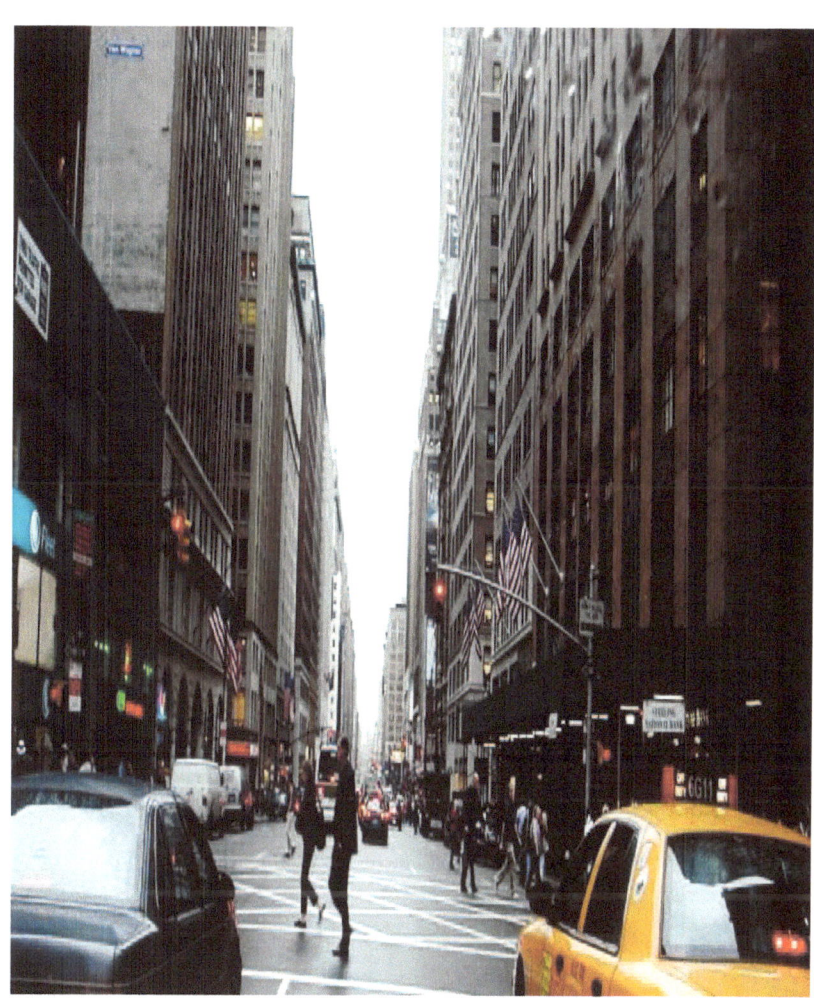

And the billboards told the story as the theaters began opening, big shiny cars daring to glide in and challenge grief itself for the city, our city, New York City.

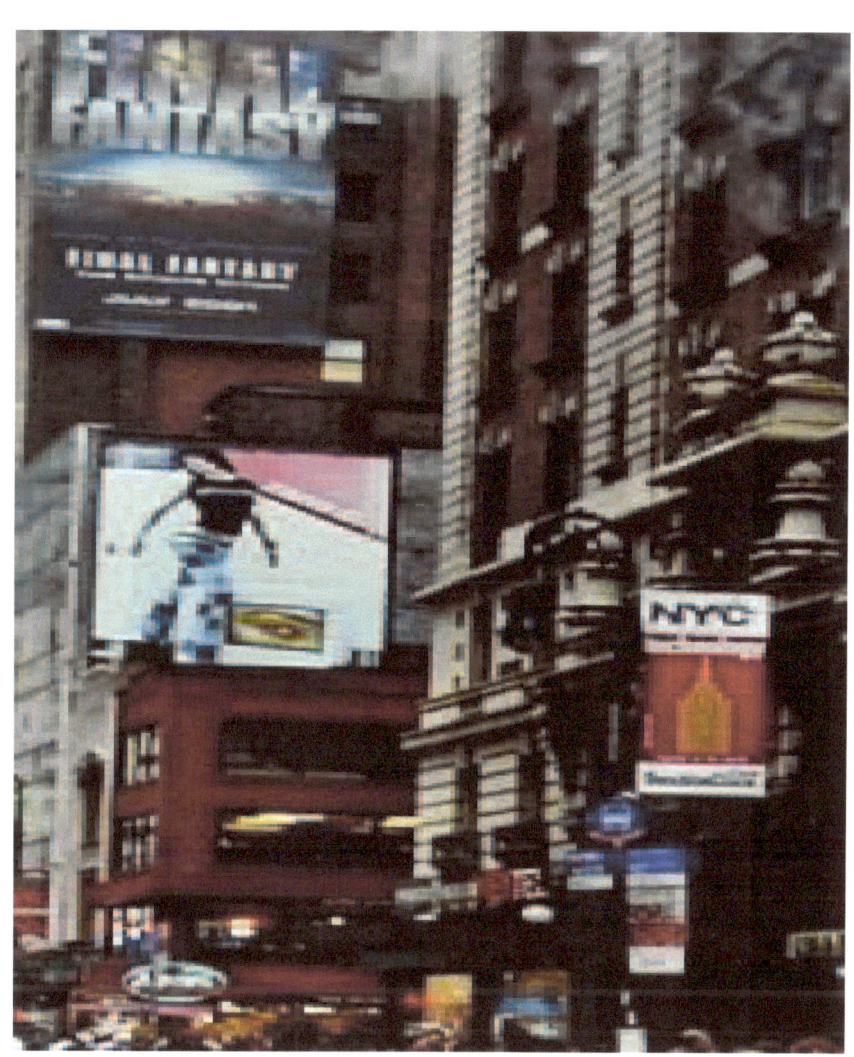

God Bless America.

God Bless New Yorkers.

God give us a promise.

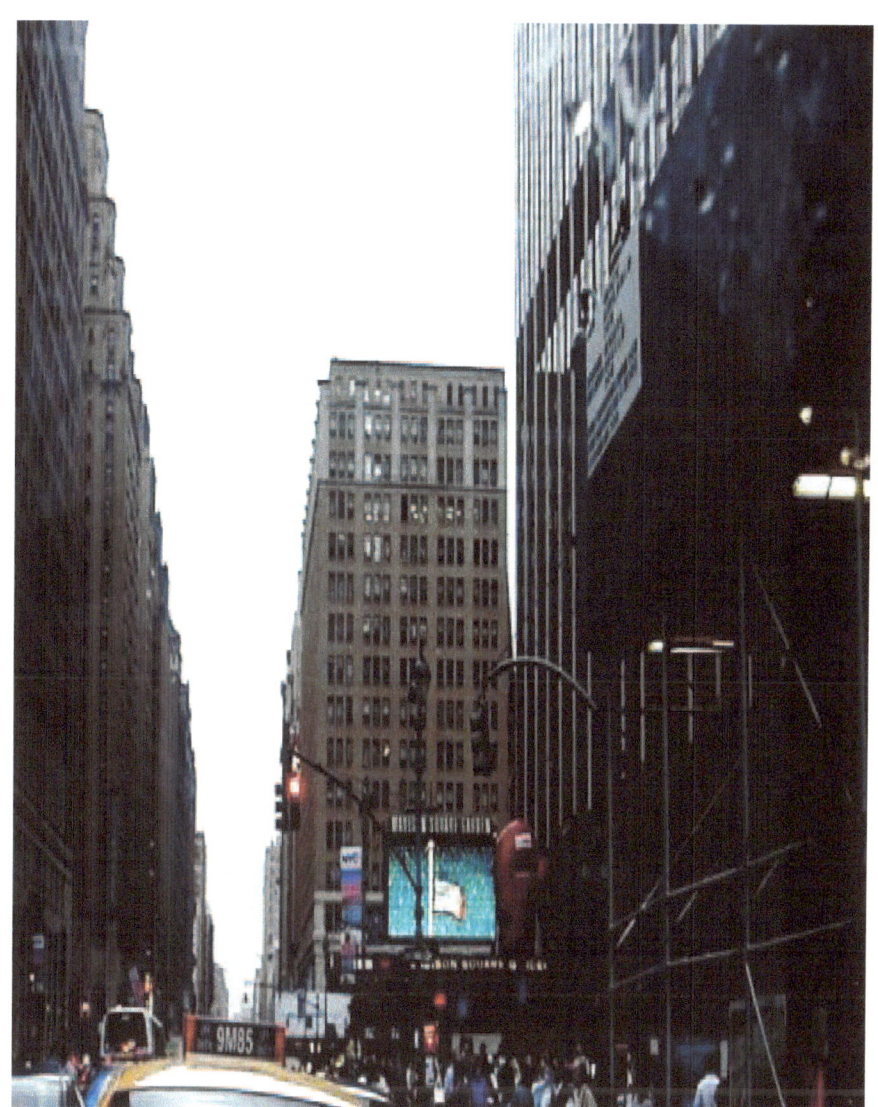

*Were the words unspoken with lights
in the sky.*

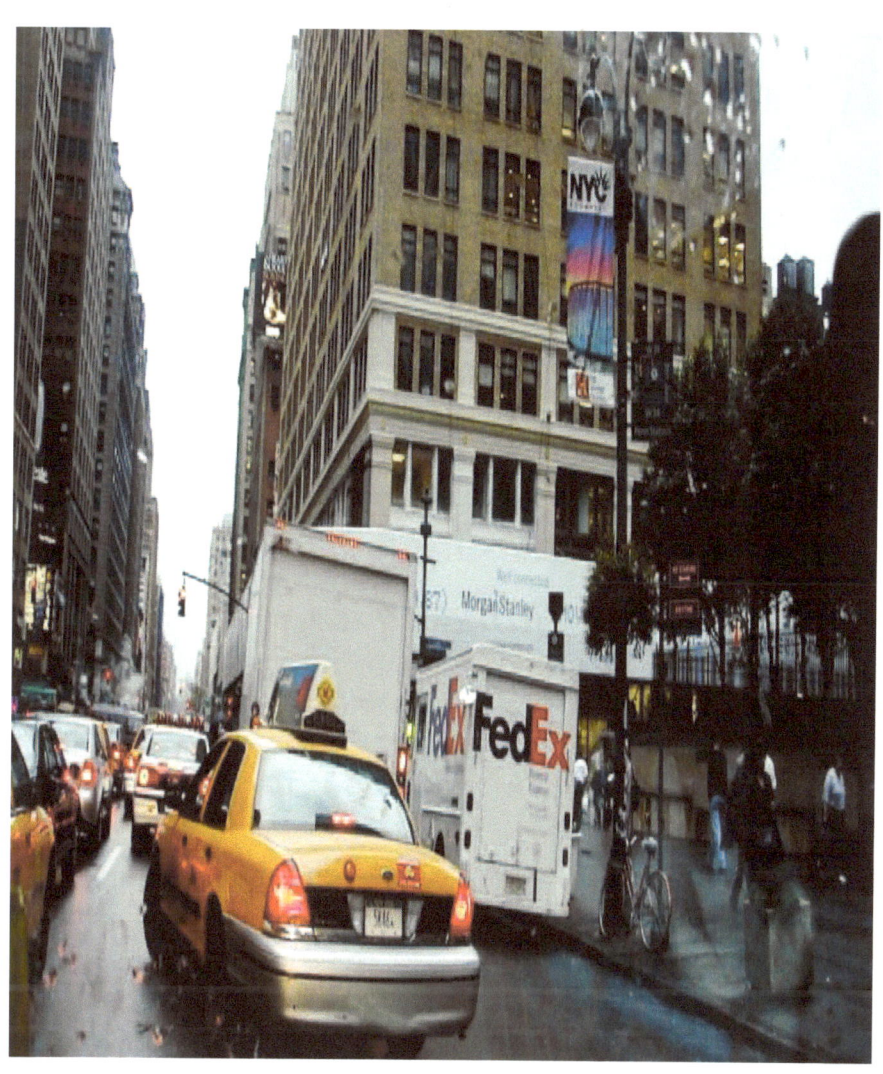

We have places to go, people to see,
things to do,

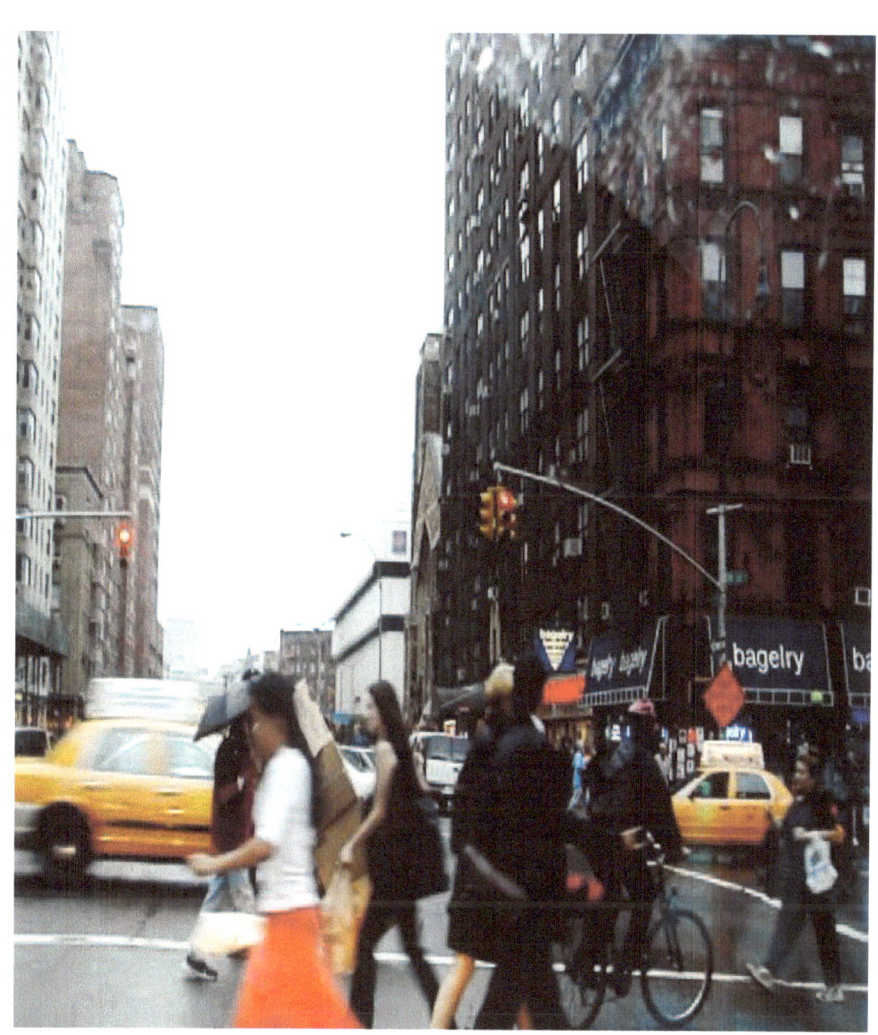

And the show must go on.

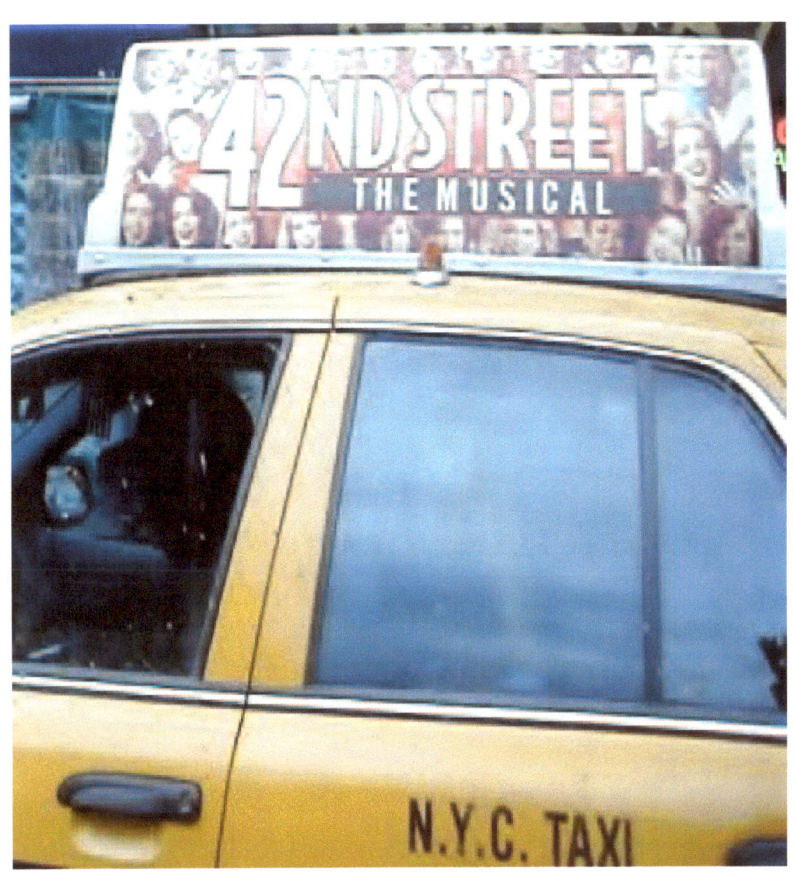

And, God forgive us, a few scores to settle.

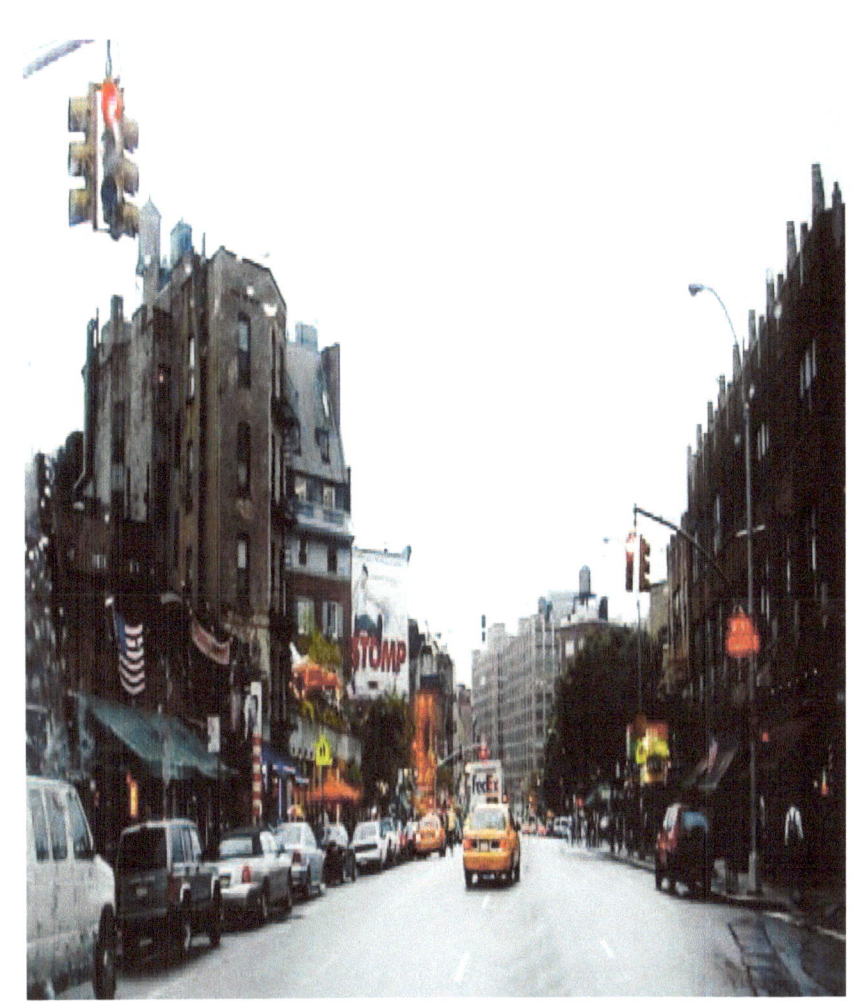

We are young, strong, and good loving
New Yorkers.

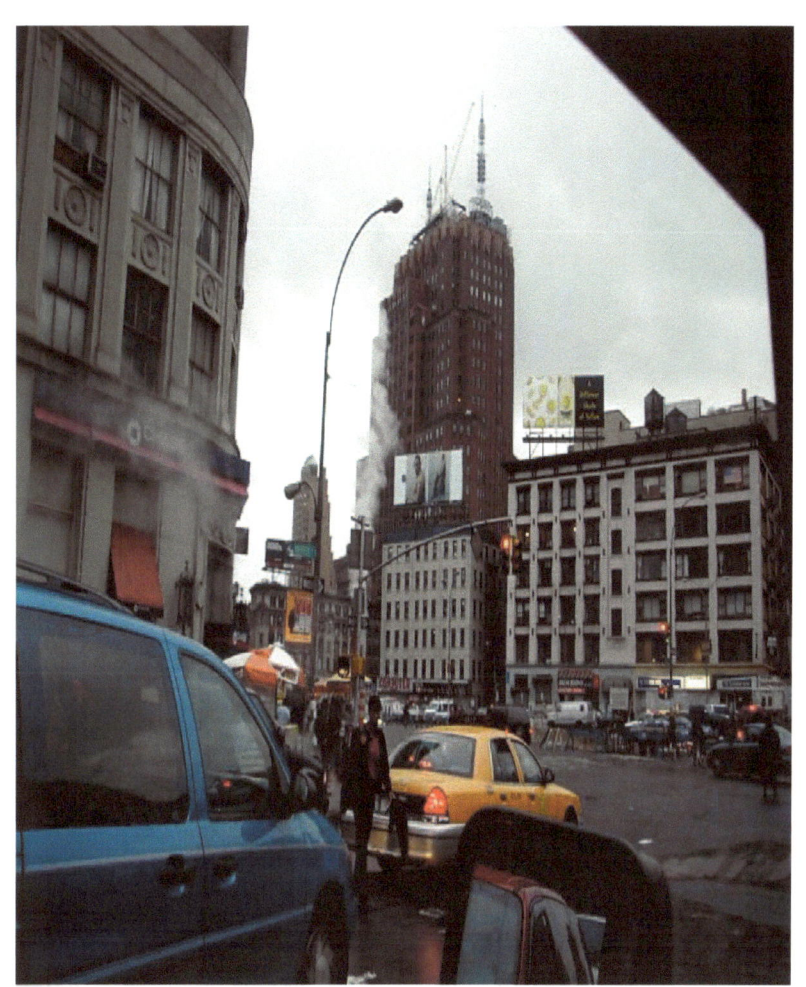

Heartache to Heartache we stand.

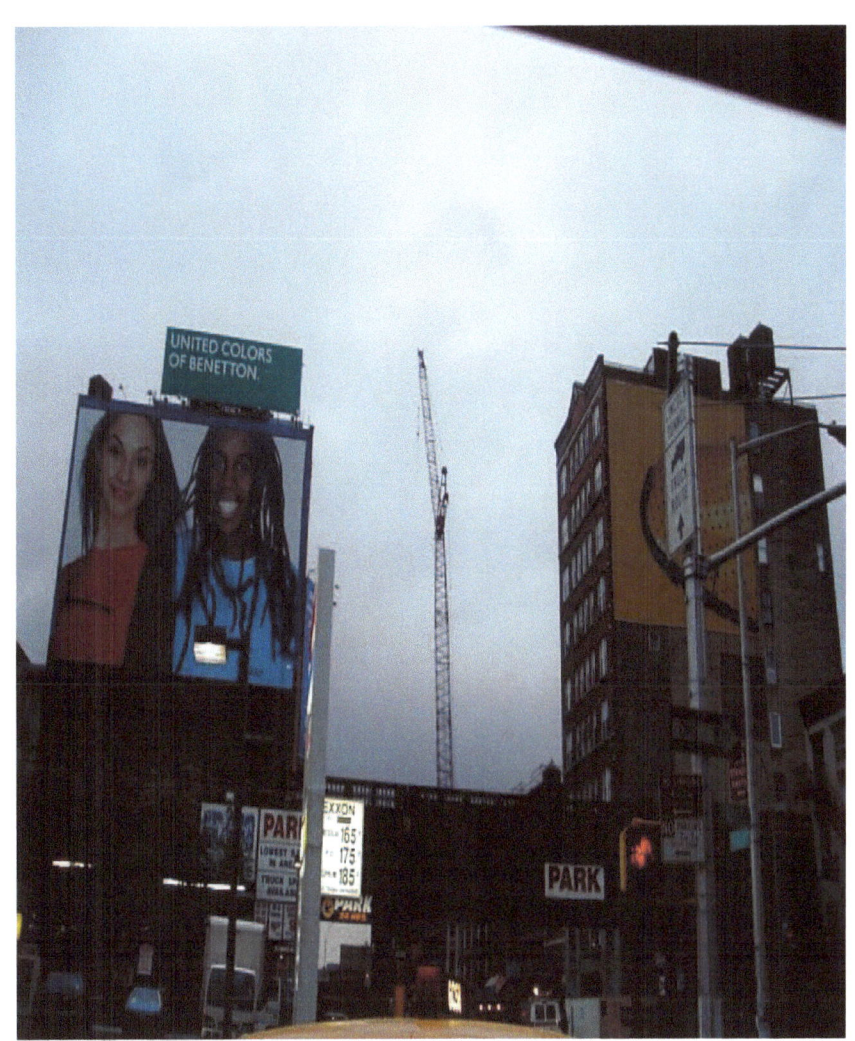

We'll pick ourselves up

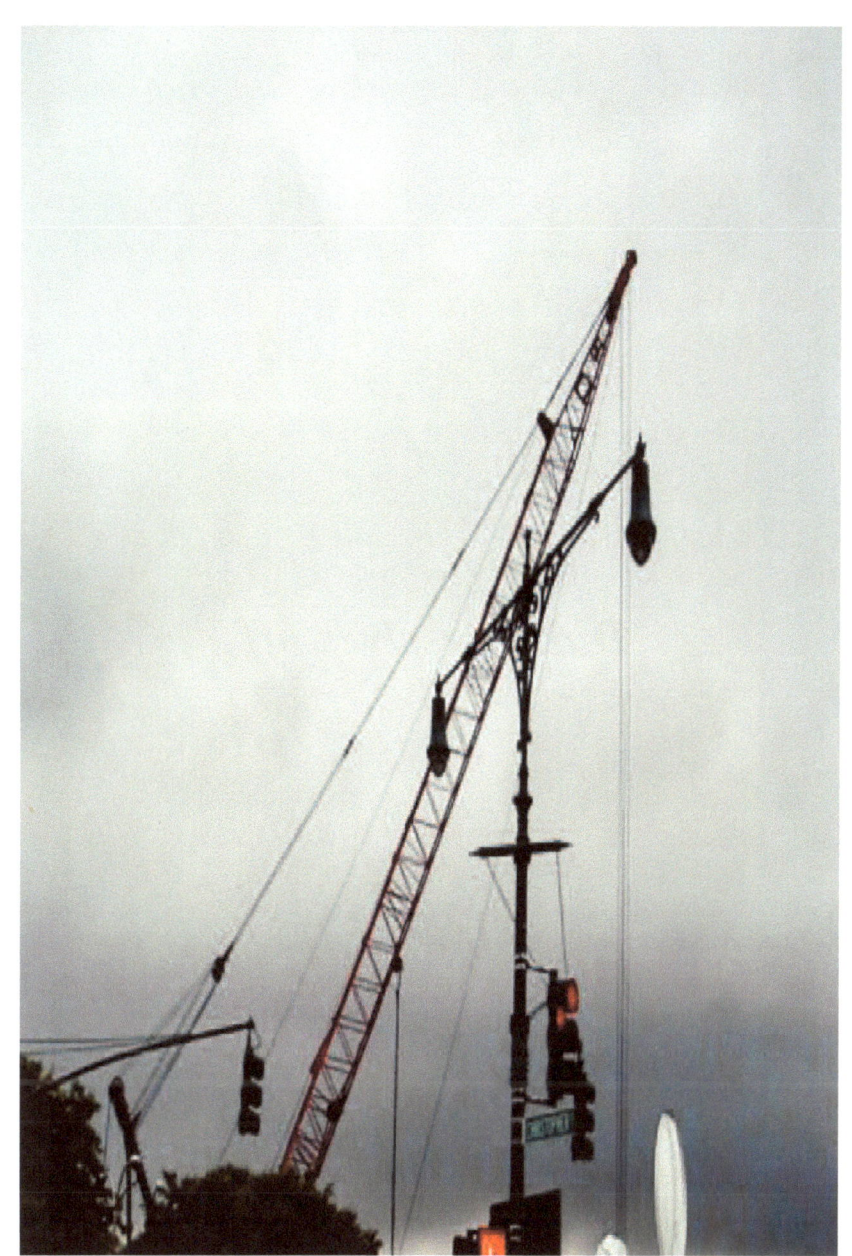

Dust ourselves off

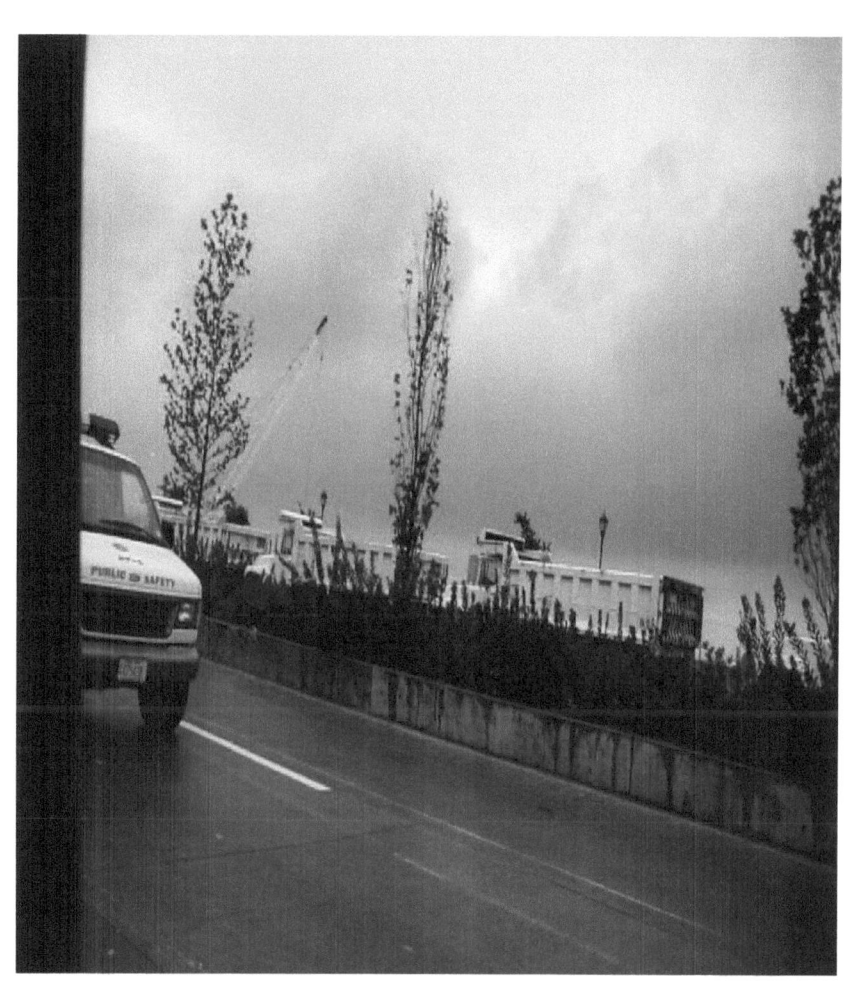

And be the freshest, juiciest Big Apple
in the world.

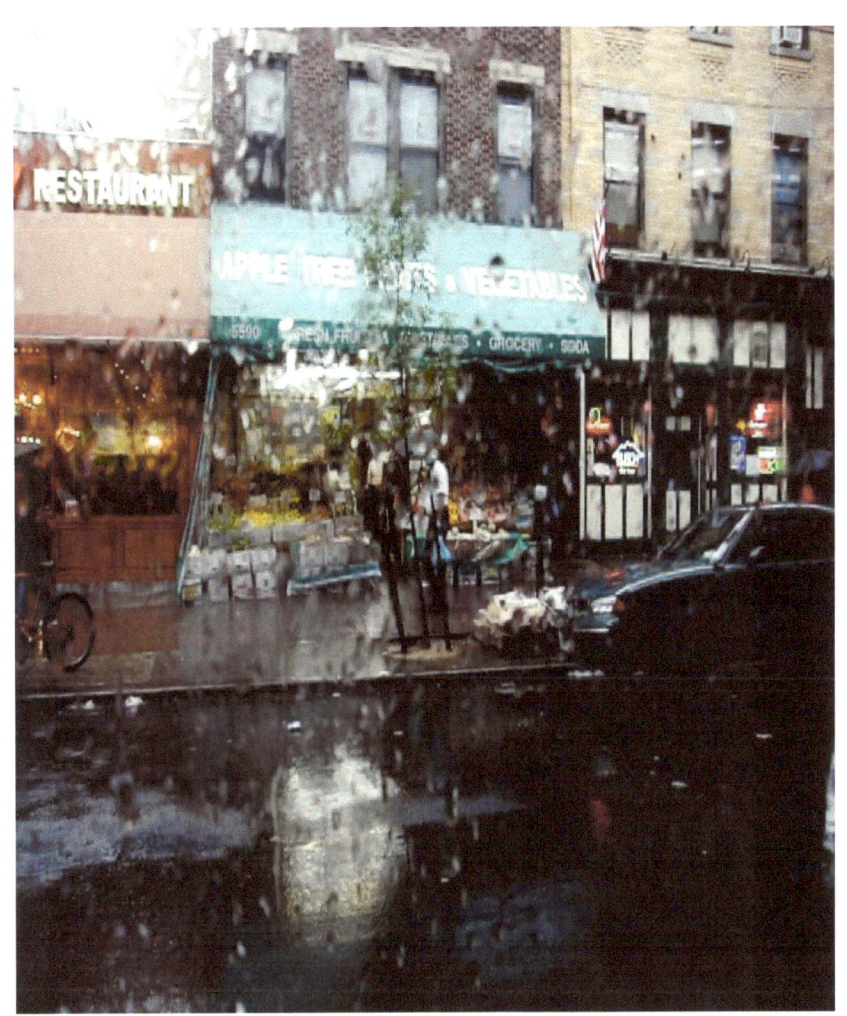

God Bless

Dedicated to those who have lost loved ones and to those brave
New Yorkers who go on.